WORCESTER COUNTY MARYLAND

WILL BOOKS LIBER JBR 1799-1803

Ruth T. Dryden

HERITAGE BOOKS
2008

HERITAGE BOOKS
AN IMPRINT OF HERITAGE BOOKS, INC.

Books, CDs, and more—Worldwide

For our listing of thousands of titles see our website at
www.HeritageBooks.com

Published 2008 by
HERITAGE BOOKS, INC.
Publishing Division
100 Railroad Ave. #104
Westminster, Maryland 21157

Copyright © 1989 Ruth T. Dryden

All rights reserved. No part of this book may be reproduced or transmitted in any form or by any means, electronic or mechanical, including photocopying, recording or by any information storage and retrieval system without written permission from the author, except for the inclusion of brief quotations in a review.

International Standard Book Numbers
Paperbound: 978-1-58549-503-0
Clothbound: 978-0-7884-7604-4

Will Book JBR Worcester Co.Md.

HANDY,Levin　　　　　　f-1,2,3
　　　　　　　　　　　　4,Jun 1798　　5 Jul 1799
　to wife____
　to four daus-Elizabeth Martin,Prisse Winder,Sarah
　　and Ester Wilson Handy (single persons)
　to brother-James Handy's children
　to brother-George Handy's daughters
　Ephraim K.Wilson, exec.
　house and lot pur/of James Morris to be sold
　wit;Betty M.Wise,John Neill,Anthony Bacon
　Ephraim K.Wilson,David Wilson,Thomas Williams gave
　bond as execs.
　　　　　　　　　　　　f-4,5
HUGHES,Jesse　　　　　　2 Sep 1798　　5 Jul 1799
　to wife-Martha,exec.
　to daus-Mary Smock, Hannah Hughes
　to sons-William,John, Jessee, James
　wit;John Taylor,Levi Merrill,Jessee Bennitt
　Martha Hughes,Levi Merrill,Levi Powell gave bond;wit.by
　Ezekiel Wise
　　　　　　　　　　　　f-6
STEVENSON,Adam　　　　　4 Jun 1796　　10 Jul 1799
　to friend-Sally Eausom(Eshom)
　wit;Anna Bishop, John Bishop
　16 Jul 1799, John Bishop,John Sturgis delivered notice
　to next of kin of Adam Stevenson dec'd that will be
　exhibited this day for probate
　　　　　　　　　　　　f-7,8,9
COLLIER,Kendal　　　　　7 Feb 1798　　27 Jul 1798
　to son-Lambert, plantation
　to dau-Molly
　to brother-Peter Collier's sons George and John
　friend-Thomas Fassitt Sr.to care for son Lambert
　to wife-Sarah, exec.
　wit;Rouse Fassitt,Reuben Cropper,Stephen Cropper
　Sarah Collier,Levin Miller,William Hudson gave bond
　　　　　　　　　　　　f-10
BREVARD,John　　　　　　13 Apr 1799　　27 Jul 1799
　to wife-Sarah, Plantation
　to dau-Nancy
　to son-Adam, pt.4 trs. MT HOPE,FRIENDSHIP,LONG RIDGE,ESEY
　to son-John, bal. of 4 trs.
　to son-Ebenezer Campbell Brevard,90a.POLKS NEGLECT adj.
　James Fassitt and George Mezick
　to son-James, bal.POLKS NEGLECT,ADDITION TO THE HEAD OF
　　MIDDLE BRACK
　to four gr.ch.-John Davis,Hetty Davis,Betsy & Sarah Davis
　wit;Nancy Cord,Edward Bredell,George Bell

                                      f-13,14
LAWRENCE,John, by word of mouth,28 Jun 1799
   on board schooner Betsy lying at Northfolk Va.,sick of
   Small pox which deceased died of in presence of Isaac
   Gray and Levin Tull on 10 Jul 1799. He leaves clothes
   to Levin Tull, $8 to Isaac Gray the Commander of Schooner
   Betsy and all prop. to Anias Tull of Worc.Co.Md.
   bonds-Hannah Tull,Isaac Tull,Levin Tull
                                  f-15,16
ROBERTS,John Sr.(Robards)   22 Feb 1797   22 Aug 1799
   to brother-Underwood Roberts, lands
   to brothers-Rencher and Thomas
   to sister-Nelly Roberts
   bro-in-law-John Roberts Jr., exec.
   wit;William Toadvine,John Ingersol,Outten Toadvine
                          f-17,18
CROPPER,Edmond Sr.   21 Jul 1799   30 Aug 1799
   to son-Edmond, lands sw/s Gavenors Branch called HOG
      QUARTER, pt.tr.MILLS NEGLECT bounds Thomas Burbage,exec.
   to son-Josiah, bal.MILLS NEGLECT, pt. ADDITION
   to son-John, tr. pur/of Edward Hammond, pt.tr.DELIGHT
      bou/of John Purnell (desc)bounds Riley Bowin & Whittington
      Bowin
   to dau-Leah Holland and dau. Sarah Rennolds
   to daus-Emila, Elizabeth, Sabrina
   son Ebenezer dec'd
   wit;James Wilson,William Cropper, McKimey Hook
   bonds with Thomas M.Purnell of W.
                              f-20
SELBY,Ann adm. of estate resigned by son William Selby
   3 Jun 1799. bond-James Selby(of John),Phillip Marsh &
   George Selby given 14 Jun 1799
                            f-20-21
HAYMAN,Nehemiah.adm. of estate refused by widow Tabitha Hayman
   and brother John Hayman Sr. but desire that Stephen Davis
   administer,1 Jun 1799. Test;John Cathell,Cornelius Riggin
   Hayman 28 Jun 1799. Robert Nairne made oath he believes
   Nehemiah Hayman has been dead 20 days.
   Bonds-Stephen Davis,John I.Purnell, Robert Nairne
                            f-22
KNOX,Solomon,late. Bond given by Joshua Hammond,Alexander
   McAllen, Henry Smock 14 Aug 1799.wit;James B.Robins
                          f-22-24
MOORE,Mary of Cecil Co.Md. 22 Apr 1799   27 Sep 1799
   to nephew-Outerbridge Horsey, exec. to have care of my
      son George W.Moore until age 21
   to son-in-law-James B.Robins and my daus. Elizabeth and
     Patty to care for 2 youngest Children, Ann Moore(under 16)
     and John Irving Moore(under 21) ment.late husband William
     Moore. I was exec. of est. of Isaac Horsey----
   nephew-Isaac Horsey, exec.,Patty Horsey, exec,James B.
     Robins,exec.
   wit;John P.Benton,Sally Welch
   bonds-Isaac Horsey,Sarah Spence, Mary Spence

F-26

STARLING, Hannah   14 Sep.1799   11 Oct.1799
    to sons- Southy and Joseph
    to dau- Hannah Evans
    wit;James Dickerson,Major Jones, Mary Jones, Levi
        Pilchard

                        f-25-26
ATKINSON,Sarah   25 Aug.1799   8 Oct.1799
    to dau- Polly
    to sons- John, Samuel, William
    Wit; William Handy,Joseph Scott, Kala Butler

                        f-28-29
WILLIAMS, Isaac   21 Sep.1799   29 Oct.1799
    to mother- Tamer Williams
    to brother- Edward Pointer Williams, RE in Sussex Co.Del.
    to bros.& sisters-Samuel, Caleb(exec),Edware P. Nancy,
        Peggy Williams
    Wit;John J. Williams,Esau Williams,Thomas N. Williams

                        f-32
WILLIAMS, Nathaniel, dec'd   21 Nov.1799
    adm. Bonds, posted by Caleb Williams, John Williams
    of Resden, Solomon Williams

                        f-34-37
MILLS,John Sr.   24 Nov.1799   24 Dec.1799
    to Pitts Creek Congregation 1 acre for Presb. Public
        meetings.
    to son-John, Plantation 99a. MILLS SECURITY, CHERRY
        STONE, bounds Thomas Hargis. Executor
    to son Levin, pt. CHERRY STONE(desc.)bounds Samuel
        McMaster
    to dau.Elizabeth
    bal. be divided equally between all my children
    wit; Hugh WIlson, Levi Ball, Gillitt Mills(gave bond)

                        f-37
DAVIS,WILLIAM,   16 Dec.1799   20 Dec.1799
    to son James
    friend- William Aydelott, exec.
    wit; Richard Rowley, John Massey,Ann Kirby; Came
    Arthur Rowley and gave bond.

3

```
                          f-39-43
GUNN,Betsy(Elizabeth)     18 Nov 1799      31 Dec 1799
    to son-Samuel, dec'd husbands watch in hands of Robert
       Atkinson
    to son-George. Kinsman Capt.George Purnell to take
       until he is 21
    to sister-Tabitha Wise
    to Sally Hudson
    Rev. Samuel McMaster to take son Samuel
    friends-Dr.John Purnell, Capt.George Purnell, execs.
    wit;Betty Wise, William Selby,George Purnell, Elisha
       Purnell, Ezekiel Wise
    bonds by-Elisha Purnell,George Selby,Zadock Sturgis
                          f-43
GREEN,Joseph, dec'd                         30 Dec 1799
    adm.bonds posted by Mary Green,John Purnell, Thomas D.
       Fassitt
                          f-44
FASSITT,James M.,dec'd                      10 Dec 1799
    adm.bonds posted by Elizabeth Fassitt, Alexander
       Franklin, Major Mumford
                          f-45
NICHOLSON,Isaac, dec'd    27 Dec 1799
    adm.bonds posted by Samuel Nicholson,John Selby,
       Nehemiah Dorman
                          f-46
MARSHALL,John D.,dec'd                      27 Dec 1799
    adm.bonds by Benjamin Wailes,Elizabeth Marshall,
       Benjamin Purnell, Robert Nairne
                       f-47-48-49
TARR,Israel               30 Mar 1799       10 Jan 1800
    to wife-Molley, plantation, then to son John, exec.
    to sons-John, Levi, James
    to dau-Sarah H.Tarr
    wit;William Smulling,Samuel A.Harper,Ephraim Matthews
    bond;Molly Tarr, Jessee Sturgis,Stephen Sturgis
                          f-50
MEZICK,George             10 Dec 1799       11 Jan 1800
    to wife-Anna, whole estate
    to dau-Sally
    to step-son-Stephen Roach
    wit;James King,Littleton Gray,Henny Bell
    bond;Ann Mezick,James King,Jessee Gray
                         f-53-55
SMITH,John                13 Nov 1799       11 Jan 1800
    to wife-Elizabeth,exec.
    to dau-Pattey Smith (minor)
    friends-John Postly, Joshua  Prideaux, guardians
    wit;Joseph Dunbar, Denny Johnson
    bond;Elizabeth Smith,Isaac Ayres,Caleb Hudson
```

```
                         f-56-58
BRATTEN,Nathaniel        12 Jan 1798     4 Feb 1800
   to wife-Comfort, 1/3rds, plantation
   to sons-Samuel, land, bounds John Brattan,John Stevens
   to son-Josiah, land, (desc), exec.
   to daus-Nancy Killam, Mary Richardson,Susannah Bishop,
      Cata Brattan
   wit;John Stevenson,Sr, Samuel Stevenson,Jacob Teague
                         f-59-64
PURNELL,John             30 Nov 1799     10 Feb 1800
   to wife-Henrietta, exec.
   to brother-George W.Purnell, exec.
   friend-Dr.John Neile, exec.
   brother-Elisha Purnell, Littleton Purnell & bro-in-law
      George Purnell trustees to sell house in Snow Hill to
      provide for my young family
   to children-Sally Purnell, John Robins Purnell
   to nephew-Thomas son of bro. Elisha
   wit;Levi Hudson,Tabitha Wise,Thomas R.P.Spence
   bonds include George Spence, Littleton Robins
                         f-65-67
MILBOURN,John            26 Jan 1800     12 Feb 1800
   to son-John, 77½acres, exec.
   to sons-Ralph and Thomas
   to daus-Pitt? Evans, Nancy Milbourne
   wit;Stephen Sturgis,John Milbourne,Jessee Sturgis,Shadrack
      Sturgis
   bonds;Thomas Dukes,Thomas Milbourne, John Milbourne
                         f-68-73
TINGLEY,Samuel           21 Jan 1799     19 Feb 1800
   (Rector of St.Partins Parish)
   to son-Samuel Johnson Tingley, 1 shilling
   to wife-Sarah, pt.land left by my father Capt.Samuel
      Tingley
   to sister-Mrs.Katharine Hall wife of Col David Hall Esq.
      of Lewis Town Deleware
   old friend Reb.Samuel Nesbits picture to his eldest son
      Samuel Nesbit residing in New York
   wit;John Benson,Michael Benson,Jesse Hudson
   bond; includes George Ross
                         f-74
TRUITT,George Sr.        13 Dec 1797     21 Mar 1800
   to wife-Elizabeth,plant.pt.MIDDLETON, land bou/o Elizab.
      Hall & Wm.Stephen Hill; timber on land bou/o Joshua
      Evans,James Brothery
   to-George Truitt s/o Outten, plant.MIDDLETON aft.wife's dec.
   to-Zadock Selby s/o Zadock, lands bou/o John Evans
   to-Sarah Truitt d/o nephew George Truitt in Kent Co.
   to-Mary Parker d/o Selby & Elizabeth w/o Selby Parker
   to-Parker & Sally ch. of Zadock Selby dec'd
   to sister-Tabitha Selby
   to-George Truitt s/o Samuel
   wit;Hugh Nilson,John O.Sturgis,Richard Sturgis
   bond;Elizabeth Truitt,Jacob Teague,Zadock Selby
```

```
                          f-78-82
JONES,Jessee              18 Mar 1800      12 Apr 1800
   to wife-Polly, lands, exec.
   to son-Handy, plant. exec. pt.ENLARGEMENT,MARTHAS PURCHSE
   to son-Jessee, my pt. of the vessell I own with Capt.
      George Spence, land called FELLOWSHIP
   to son-Riley, land where John Heather formerly lived
   to daus-Rebeccah and Charlotte
   wit;Phillip Moris,Eli Bowen,James Wilson
   bonds include,James B.Robins, Barzilla S.Parker
                          f-83
TOWNSEND,Lazarus          12 Mar 1799      30 May 1800
   to wife-Mary
   to dau-Sally
   wit;Thomas Mitchell, McKimmy Hook
                          f-84-85
HORSEY,Lambert            16 Dec 1798      27 Jun 1800
   to nephew-Revil Horsey
   to sister-Zipporah Bruff, exec.
   wit;Edward Henry,Joshua Prideaux, Nathaniel Brittingham
                          f-86-88
PRICE,Arthur              3 Jun 1800       27 Jun 1800
   to sons-John M___Price and Peter, lands,(desc)
   to son-Arthur, 50a. where Michael Tarr lives
   to son-William, bal. of land
   to wife-Sarah, and Ezekiah Johnson, execs.
   wit;James Willia,Hezekiah Johnson,Elisha Johnson
   bonds include-James Selby,Jabez Brumbly
                          f-89-92
COLLIER,Layfield          20 Jun 1800      5 Aug 1800
   to mother-Tabitha Collier
   to wife-Sally, 1/3rds
   to dau-Molly White Collier
   to-Isaac Hill's two sons,Stephen & Elijah Hill
   wit;Josiah Mitchell,James A.Collier,Josiah Hill
   bond-Thomas N.Williams,Edward Henry,Jacob White
                          f-93-98
FASSITT,James Mumford     unisgned,no date 11 Jan 1800
   to wife-Elizabeth,plant.where John Jones lives 200a.
   to-sister's son John Collier
   to brother John
   wit;Constant Mariner and Comfort his wife,John Fassitt Jr,
      Elizabeth Fassitt
   1 Jan 1799 deposition of Wm.Fassit-wrote will shortly
      after and that James died in month of August last.
   Disposition of Catherine Collier-in July James M.Fassitt
      wrote his will and left all prop to wife
   Dispositions taken of Major Mumford,Samuel Quillan,
      Priscilla Massey
   Articles of agreement;12 Feb 1800 by Ephraim Wilson on
      behalf of John Fassitt,Constand Mariner & Comfort,John
      Mumford and Sally his wife on one part and John Dennis,
      Stephen Purnell and Goerge Ross for Elizabeth Abbits
      Fassitt on the other part
   Bonds;Elizab.Fassitt,Laban Johnson,Major Mumford
```

                              f-98-100
GUNN,Henry   20 Jul 1800   11 Aug 1800
    to wife-Mary
    to son-George, land my bro.Levin Gunn b/o Col.Peter Chaile
    to son-Henry,lands (boht sons under 21)
    to son-George, 50a. SMITHS CHOICE (desc)
    to daus-Elizabeth Clarke,Rebekah Gunn,Mary Gunn
    wit;James Smith,Thomas Dixon,William Smith
    bond includes John Gillett
                              f-101-104
DAVIS,Mathias   15 Aug 1800   29 Aug 1800
    to son-Littleton, lands. exec.
    to nephews-Benjamin and Isaac sons of bro.Abijah
    to wife-Betty
    wit;William Whittington,Ephraim K.Wilson,John C.Kennerly,
        Levin Pollitt
                              f-105
PARTICK,John, dec'd   11 Feb 1800
    adm.bonds by Sarah Patrick,Stephen White,Layfield Collier
                              f-106
WELL,Thomas, dec'd   11 Feb 1800
    adm.bonds by Polly Well,Americus Powell, Elijah
    Brittingham, Jacob White
                              f-107
TINGLE,Elijah, dec;d   11 Feb 1800
    adm.bonds by Daniel Tingle,Layfield Collier,John Tingle
                              f-108
PURNELL,John Selby, dec'd   11 Feb 1800
    adm.bonds by Lanta Purnell,Littleton Robins,George Purnell
                              f-109
DIXON,Mary, dec'd   10 Mar 1800
    adm.bonds by Phillip Quinton,Wm.Quinton,Samuel Nicholsen
                              f-110
HULL,Richard, dec'd   11 Mar 1800
    adm.bonds by Catherine Hull,Nathaniel Bowen,John Bowen
                              f-110
WRIGHT,John, dec'd   14 Mar 1800
    adm.bonds by John Bishop,Allanta Wright,Zadock Sturgis,
        Jacob Teague
                              f-112
ROWND,John H.   9 Apr 1800
    adm.bonds by Richard Henry Handy, Capt.Thomas Handy,
        John P.Marshall
                              f-113
ROWND,Peggy Winder,dec;d   9 Apr 1800
    adm.bonds by Richard H.Handy,Capt.Thos.Handy,John P.Marhsall
                              f-114
MARTIN,Rosannah, dec'd   12 Jun 1800
    adm.bonds by Thomas Martin,James Martin,Dr.John Neill
                              f-115
NICHOLSON,Joseph, dec'd   11 Apr 1800
    adm.bonds by Samuel Nicholson,Isaac Cottingham,Samuel Handy

```
                    f-116
GUNN,Samuel, dec'd                      9 May 1800
    adm.bonds by George Purnell,ZadockSturgis,Patrick Waters
                    f-117
DAVIS,James, dec'd                      10 Jun 1800
    adm;bonds by Ezekiel Davis,Robert Hudson,Nathaniel Bowen
                    f-118
JACOBS,Nimrod,dec'd                     10 June 1800
    adm.bonds by Elizaeth Holland,John Holland,John Selby
                    f-119
HOLLAND,Thomas, dec'd                   10 Jun 1800
    adm.bonds by Elizabeth Holland,John Holland,John Selby
                    f-120
BRATTAN, John S.                        19 Apr 1800
    I Mary M.Bratten widow of John S.Brattan refuse adm.
    adm.bonds by George Rice,John Rock,John C.Handy 7 July
                    f-121
STEVENS,Eliner, dec'd                   25 Jul 1800
    adm.bonds by George Ross,Thomas Handy,Capt.James Broadwater
                    f-122
STEVENSON,Jonathan, dec;d               13 Aug 1800
    adm.bonds by Lydia Stevenson,Wm.Stevenson,Joseph Stevenson
                    f-123-125
QUINTON,Phillip         23 Oct 1797     26 Sep 1800
    to wife-Esther, Exec.
    to gr.dau-Comfort Quinton Gore
    to children,-William,Phillip,Littlcton,Isaac,Esther,Sarah
    wit;Zadock Sturgis,John Bishop,Thomas Mitchell
                    f-126-131
PURNELL,Elisha          10 Feb 1800     19 Sep 1800
    to wife-Mary, lands exec.
    to daus-Martha,Mary,Sarah and Elizabeth
    to son in law-James Trip and John Purnell
    to gr.sons-Elisha Purnell, Jepthat Purnell Marshall(under21)
    wit;Esme Purnell,Milby Purnell, James Houston Jr.
                    f-132
ELMORE,John, dec'd                      30 Sep 1800
    Comfort Laws late Comfort Elmore,Thomas Jones,Peter Parker
                    f-133
REDDEN,Leah             9 Sep 1800      14 Oct 1800
    to son-John and his son Stephen
    to sons-Shadrack, Stephen
    to dau-Mary
    to sons-Nehemiah and James, 1 shilling each
    wit;James Dickerson,Jonathan Melvin,Sarah Melvin,gavebonds
```

```
                            f-138-142
BEVANS,Jane              25 Aug 1800      11 Oct 1800
   (wife of Rowland Bevans, by virture of my marriage con-
   tract bearing date of 21 Mar 1795)
   to gr.daus-Charlotte & Sally Maddux
   to daus-Hannay Poynter, Bathesheba Bevans
   to gr.dau.-Jean Poynter
   to son-Jacob Richard, exec.
   to gr.sons-Joseph Richards, Nathaniel Richards
   son-in-law-Mills Bevans, exec.
   wit;William Handy, Taby Bevans
   bonds include-Capt.Geo.Purnell,John Bishop 14 Oct 1800
                            f-143-150
LAYFIELD,Isaac           7 Sep 1800       11 Oct 1800
   to son-Thomas,plantation HOG QUARTER(desc)near Cypress
      Swamp bounds John Whittington,John D.Marshall heirs,
      300a. CYPRESS SWAMP (minor)
   to gr.son-Isaac Layfield, plantation where James Merrill
      lives, MILLERS LOTT bounds widow Betty Henderson, 200a.
      CYPRESS SWAMP
   to wife-Esther, 1/3rds, exec.
   to daus-Elizabeth Sneed,Nancy Layfield, Catty Barrett
   dec'd_dau. Mary Patterson
   wit;Littleton Dennis,Zadock Wheeler,Esau Boston
   bonds include,Joseph Henderson,Anderson Patterson
                            f-151-152
GIVEN,John Mc., dec'd                     14 Oct 1800
   adm.bonds by John Bohannon,John Ayres, Zadock Selby
                            f-153-158
MARTIN,Thomas            22 Aug 1800      28 Oct 1800
   to wife-Anna Bishop, 5½a. PUZZLE, and prop. she had at
      the time of our marriage
      land, ACQUANTICO SAVANNAH to be sold.
   to daus-Leah Martin, Sarah Wise, house, 50a.and wood from
      tr. SELBYS SECURITY
   to son-Thomas, tr.SELBYS SECURITY, KILLAMS CHOICE
   to gr.children-Sarah Martin d/o Wm.my son,bal.of DUMLANDING
      Susan and Sarah Martin daus/o son George, Molly Martin
      d/o son Levin, Molly & William Wise children of dau.
      Sarah Wise
   10a.adj.land of James Duer bou/of McKimmy Scarborough pt.
      tr.MARDYKE, to be sold called DUMLANDING
   to nephew-Thomas Martin
   to children-Thomas and Leah, lands on the beach bou/o
      Benjamin Dennis
   brother-James Martin, friend Col.Samuel Handy, nephew
      Thomas Martin execs.
   wit;Samuel R.Smith,Mary H.Martin,Charlotte H.Martin
   9 Nov 1800 James Martin & Samuel Handy rejject adm.
   bonds-Thomas Martin Esq.,Robert M.Richardson,Dr.John Neill
```

```
                              f-159-165
SPENCE,George                 no date              28 Oct 1800
    to wife-Nancy, lands, timber land pur/o William Purnell
      trustee of Thomas Richardson; use of plantation where
      William Hook lived until son John is 21yrs.,exec.
    to son-Adam, pt.tr.SNOW HILL, bounds Rev.David Balls,
      James Handy and wife (desc)
    to son-Thomas Robins Purnell Spence, lot in Snow Hill #20
    to son-Lemuel Purnell Spence, lands at Calkers Creek
    to son-John Spence,(under 21) SMITHS FIRST CHOICE where
      William Hook lately lived
    to son-William, lands n/e of James Selby's plant where
      Old Charles now lives, lands on Rattlesnake Island,
      ½ of lot #5 in Snow Hill
    to son-James Robins Spence, pt. of SNOW HILL CONFIRMATION
      bounds Snow Hill bridge, Pocomoke River, Brewhouse
      landing, Paddy's Bridge; COLEMANS HORNS
    to son-Ara Spence, plantation now held by James Handy &
      wife where Ralph Holstone lives (see desc)
    to son-George, plantation & woodland where I.live
    to dau-Betsy Washington Spence, ½ of lot #5 in Snow Hill
      where Robert Smith now lives
    to dau-Andasia Spence, lands, bounds James Selby, DOVER,
      Mt EPHRAIM,Levi Richardson,James Brattan (desc)
    lands on Asseteague Beach MIDDLE MORE to sons equally
    George Purnell and James B.Robins to advise family
    John S.Purnell, exec.
    wit;James B.Robins,John Purnell, Elisha Purnell
    bonds include Littleton Purnell
                              f-166-170
TOWNSEND,Levin                24 Sep 1800          25 Nov 1800
    to son-(not yet Christened)to be called Teagle Townsend,
      lots in Snow Hill #9 & 10, at age 21
    to wife-Ann, lot where I live, exec.
    to daus-Nancy and Sarah
    John Cottingham Esq. exec. (rejects adm)
    wit;Silvanus Uriah Roberts, John Riggen,John Dorman
    bonds-Ann Townsend,Capt.Thomas R.Handy,James Adkinson
                              f-171-5
GILLETTE,William              16 Dec 1800          25 Dec 1800
    to daus-Anna, Wealthey Gillett, plantion(desc) bounds
      Levi Ball,Elijah Townsend, Major Davis
    to wife-Elizabeth, exec.
    John Logan, exec.
    wit;Rachel Taylor,Jarman Taylor
    Elizabeth Gillette rejects adm.(ill and cannot attend myself)
    bonds-John Logan,Samuel McMaster,Joseph Stevenson Sr.
                              f-176
DOWNS,Sarah                   5 Jan 1800           17 Oct 1800
    to sister-Margaret Downs
    to brother-Mitchell Down's son Robert Downs
    to-Gertrude Purnell's children
    David Wilson, exec
    wit;Gertrude Purnell, Euphamia Purnell
```

```
                         f-178
BEAVANS,Jememia         16 Sep 1800      27 Nov 1800
   to-sister Sarah Mills widow of Stephen
   to-Mary Bevans daughter of Benjamin
   to-Esther Tilghman wife of Ephraim
   Ephraim Tilghman, exec.
   wit;Henry Townsend, Isacah Tilghman
                         f-179
WALTON,Nancy, word of mouth on           16 Nov 1800
   this will just frees her negros
   wit;Fisher W.Richardson,Sally Richardson,Vollentine Dennis
                         f-180
GRAY,Johnson, dec'd                      14 Oct 1800
   adm.bonds by Martha Gray,James King,Thomas Gray
                         f-181
PURNELL,Azariah, dec'd                   28 Oct 1800
   adm.bonds by Mary Purnell widow of Azariah, John Davis,
   John Richards        f-182
DAVIS,Abijah, dec'd                      31 Oct 1800
   adm.bonds by Littleton Davis,Levin Pollitt,John C.Handy
                         f-182
ATKINSON,Robert, dec'd  29 Nov 1800
   Am ill, cannot adm. on brother Roberts est.-Thomas Atkinson
   bonds by-James Atkinson,Wheatly Dennis,George Hayward
                         f-183
WALTON,John, dec'd                       2 Jan 1801
   adm.bonds by John Selby of Parker,Isaac Ayres,Wm.Corbin
                         f-184
BRITTINGHAM,Solomon, dec'd               9 Jan 1801
   adm.bonds by Isaac Brittingham,Dr.George Purnell, Samuel
   Ennis                f-185
WATERS,Patrick, dec'd                    23 Jan 1801
   adm.bonds by Esther Waters,Peter Waters,John Ayres,
     Frederick Conner
                         f-186
PURNELL,Elisha, dec'd                    9 Jan 1800
   adm.bonds by Mary Purnell, John Ayres,John Purnell
                         f-187-188
BOWEN,Joshua            3 Nov 1800       11 Jan 1801
   (on board Sloop Washington at anchor at Reedy Island)
   to son-Joshua, tract where family lives
   wife-Betsy (pregnant)exec. and her bro. Thomas Hall, exec.
   to four ch-John, Hetty,Caty and Joshua
   two vessells I own to be sold
   wit;Johnson Durham, George Hall, John Bishop
   bonds-Thomas Hall, Purnell Porter, George Hall
```

                            f-189-191
NICHOLSON,Samuel   27 Dec 1800   16 Jan 1801
   to neice-Nancy Nicholson d/o brother Isaac
   to neices & nephews,-John, Betsy, Peter,Elisha, James
      children of brother William Dickerson
   friend-Joseph Houston Sr. be guardian of neice Nancy
      Nicholson until she is age 16
   friends-William Quinton, William Selby execs.& witnesses
   bonds include-Robert Handy, Phillip Quinton
                            f192-193
RICHARDSON,Levi   3 Dec 1800   28 Jan 1801
   to children-Sarah Richardson, Levi Richardson
   if Sarah should marry Littleton Mumford then all to son
   nephew-Joseph Richardson guardian
   wit;Jacob Teague,Josiah Brattan,Benjamin Richardson
   codicil-Joseph Richardson to deed parcel of land to
      Capt.George Spence 23 Dec 1800
                            f-194-196
GORNELL, Major   30 Dec 1800   26 Jan 1801
   to daus-Sally Outten Gornell, Mary Gornell (minors)
   Elijah Richards guardian
   wit;William Deverix, Littleton Robins
   bonds, Elijah Richards,Thomas Mitchell,John K.Truitt
                            f-197
TRUITT,Rownds   19 Jan 1797   30 Jan 1801
   to wife-Levinar
   to son-James, bal. of that land against Benjamin Truitt
   to daus-Anna Godfrey, Lotte Truitt
   wit;Curtis Henderson,Selby Parker
   bonds include Joshua Brittingham
                            f-198-200
HENDERSON,Purnell   22 Jan 1801   12 Feb 1801
   to sons-Isaac, John, Thomas
   todau-Nancy Henderson
   friend- Ananias German, exec.
   wit;Isaac Richards,Nehemiah Truitt,Levin Derickson
   bonds include, Erasmus Harrison
                            f-201
PHILLIPS,Isaac, dec'd   10 Feb 1801
   Ruth Phillips widow of Isaac renounces exec. and gives to
      son Joshua Phillips
   bond by Joshua Phillips, Cornelius Morris,Avery Bradford
                            f-202
POWELL,John,dec'd   13 Feb 1801
   adm.bonds by Jessee Powell,Abisha Davis,Erasmus Harrison
                            f-203-205
POWELL,Belitha   13 Dec 1800   13 Feb 1801
   to-brother John Powell's children, Esther,Molly, John,
      lands and to their mother Keziah Powell 1/4th pt.
   pt. CYPRESS SWAMP bou/o Richard Sampson to be sold
   to sister-Sally Bradford wife of John
   cousin-Jessee Powell, exec.
   wit;John Postly,Erasmus Harrison,Samuel McCrea
   bonds include, Abisha Davis

```
                       f-206
TURPIN, John, dec'd                      14 Feb 1801
   adm.bonds by John J.Williams,Isaac Ayres,Thomas N.Williams
                       f-207
VEAZEY,Thuzey (Louthy)    24 Feb 1801     3 Mar 1801
   to dau-Sally and son Samuel Veazey
   wit;John Handcock
                       f-208
STEVENSON,Nanny           17 Sep 1798     5 Mar 1801
   to daus-Nicy Johnson
   to sons-Jabez Stevenson, Thomas Stevenson,exec.
   wit;Elizabeth Wright,Moses M.Greer,George Purnell
                       f-209-211
HILL,Levin Sr.            18 Dec 1800    13 Mar 1801
   to daus-Levinia Hill, Betsy Pruitt
   to brother-Frederick Hill
   to son-Levin,lands (desc) pt. tr.ROBERTSONS INHERITANCE,
      ADDITION TO WILLETTS OUTLET, then to his son Frederick
   to son-Purnell Hill, bal. of ROBERTS INHERITANCE & WILLETTS
      OUTLET
   to housekeeper-Mary Parker
   to- Peter White
   to gr.dau-Peggy Hill
   friend-Jessee Bennett trustee
   wit;Joshua Sturgis,Stephen Allen,Thomas Taylor
                       f-212-213
HANDY,John, Capt. dec'd                  13 Mar 1801
   (one of the nephews of William Allen Esq, dec'd)
   it is our desire James Bacon Esq. should adm.estate;signed
      Jacob Handy, George Ross,Thomas Martin,Francis Ross
   bonds by-James Bacon,Col.Samuel Handy, McKimmy Porter
                       f-214-216
NEWTON,Levin              5 May 1799     27 Mar 1801
   to wife-Sarah, plantation, exec.
   to dau-Comfort Newton, ½ lands, plant.after wife's death
   to daus-Polly, Sally, Charlotte
   to dau-Nancy, ½ of plant. after mothers death
   to- my supposed son Josiah Newton, 1 shilling
   wit;John Houston,George Houston,Jessee Bennett
   bonds include, Purnell Hill, Laban Hudson
                       f-217
HALL,Elizabeth            23 Nov 1798    31 Mar 1801
   to gr.son-John H.Hill, 148a. land
   to gr.sons-Jessee Hill, William S.Hill
   to gr.daus-Betsey Brittingham Hill, Nancy Hill
   wit;Handy Mills,David Smith,Stephen Sturgis
                       f-218-220
POWELL,Thomas             24 Jan 1776     April 1801
   (19 Dec 1900 will transfered from Ann Arundel Co.Md.)
   to-John Dale,inspector, 8a.pt.POWELLS PURCHASE (desc)if
      he conveys to my heirs 8a. of SECOND ADDITION
   to-Thomas Dale son of John
   to cousin-John Powell s/o Samuel
   to cousin-Esther Pitts dau/of Samuel Powell and her husband
      H,llary Pitts, lands, POWELLS PURCHASE
   friend-John Postly, exec.
   wit;Solomon Baker,Mathias Davis,James Dale
                          13
```

```
                         f-221
PENNEWELL,John, dec'd                      28 Mar 1801
   widow Rachel Pennewell renounces, has no child old
   enough to do it. Appts. Elijah Brittingham adm.
   adm.bonds by,Elijah Brittingham,Isaac Ayres,John Davis
                         f-222
VEZEY,Charles            24 Jan 1801      9 Jul 1801
   to wife-Mary
   wit;John Handcock
                         f-223
BRADSHAW,Morgan, dec'd                     9 Jun 1801
   adm.bonds, Arthur McAllen,Alexander McAllen,Richard Sturgis
                         f-224-5
LAWS,Comfort             28 Apr 1801      9 Jun 1801
   to dau-Mary Parker
   to gr.sons-James Parker son of Peter Parker and Joshua
      Jones
   to sons-James Jones, John Jones
   to gr.daus-Comfort Parker,Elizabeth Walton Parker
   son-in-law-Peter Parker, exec.
   wit;Isaac Hill,Elijah Brittingham
   bonds include, Zadock Sturgis,John Townsend
                         f-226-228
HENDERSON,Jacob          18 Dec 1800      25 Jul 1801
   to wife-Elizabeth, ½ land MY OLD PLACE, exec.
   to dau-in-law-Easher Henderson (widow)
   to gr.dau-Aary Henderson, ½ lands
   friends-Levi Henderson,James Henderson, trustees
   wit;Stephen Roach,Edward Lambden,Samuel Merrill
                         f-229-231
MITCHELL,Josiah          1 Aug 1797       11 Aug 1801
   to son-Joshua, tr.MITCHELLS CONCLUSION n/s road from
      COYES FOLLY to St.Martins church
   to dau-Ann Mitchell
   to son-Levin, bal.of MITCHELLS CONCLUSION on SE/side of rd.
   to sons-Joshua and Levin, pt. tr.STRABAN bou/of William
      Ironshire 322a.
   to daus-Elizabeth Hill, Mary Rock
   wit;William Covington,Daniel Tingle,Ananias Powell
                         f-232-233
FRANKLIN,William         ___ ___1800      12 Aug 1801
   to wife-Sarah, lands, exec.
   to daus- Comfort and Elizabeth Cammell
   to sons-Ebenezer and Robert
   to son-in-law-William Burton
   wit;Samuel Pile,Levin Turner,John Church
   (will prob. Philadelphia 12 Jan 1801
   bonds-Sarah Franklin,William Dale,Jacob White
                         f-234
DAVIS,Charles, dec'd                      12 Aug 1801
   adm.bonds-Nancy Davis,Peter S.Corbin,Nehemiah Holland,
      William Holland
```

```
                         f-235
ELMORE,John, dec'd                        13 Aug 1801
   adm.bonds by John Richards, James Hineman
                         f-236
FRANKLIN, Ebenezer, dec'd                 13 Aug 1801
   adm.bonds by Isaac Franklin,James Franklin,Peter Evans
                         f-237-240
POWELL,Thomas Sr.        2 Aug 1789       28 Aug 1801
   to gr.son-Elisha Powell,37a.pt.POWELLS SECURITY (desc)
      WILD CAT DEN 87a.
   to son-Thomas, bal.of POWELLS SECURITY between Zadock's
      and Elisha's parts, 110a.
   to son-Annanias, pt.POWELLS SECURITY, bounds, tree marked
      by Rachel Powell for William Harrison
   to son-Jessee, pt.same, 8a. RACHELS LOTT where I now
      live that my bro.Samuel Powell alienated to me
   to four daus-Elizabeth Powell(others not named)
   to gr.son-Milby Powell and the children of dau.Rachel
      Davis dec'd.
   wit;Benjamin McCormack, Belitha Powell, Jessee Gray
      (dec'd by 1801)    (dec'd by 1801)
   4 Sept 1801-Ananias Powell renounces exec. to brother
      Jessee Powell
   bonds include, William Richards, Levi Dorman
                         f-241-245
REDDEN,John              20 Nov 1800       4 Sep 1801
   to son-John,plantation MULBERRY HEATH deeded from
      Joshua Guthrey 94a., 21a.bou/o Solomon Pepper,
      St.LEONARDS
   to son-William
   to son-Nehemiah, 50a. MULBERRY HEATH deeded by Willima
      Pepper,Annie Pepper, John Pepper to Christopher Glass,
      6a. TOBIAS DISSAPPOINTMENT
   to son-Stephen, tr.MIFFLINS PARTNERSHIP bou/o Hope Taylor
   to son- Peter, lands in Pitts Creek hundred 160a.
   to daus-Eleanor,Hetty and Sally Handcock
   to Malthy Beachboard
   son-in-law-Daniel Handcock, exec.
   wit;John Holland,Michael Tarr, Betsy Hader
   4 Aug 1801 codicil; to wife Sarah, plantation for 4 yrs
      no longer.
   to son-John 12 a. lately taken up
   wit;John Bonnewell
   bonds-Stephen Redden,Daniel Handcock,John Holland
                         f-246
NICHOLSON,Isaac,dec'd                     4 Sep 1801
   adm.bonds-William Selby,Wm.Quinton,John C.Handy,Joseph Houston
                         f-247-8
HUTSON,John              20 May 1801       4 Nov 1801
   to wife-Polly (Mary)exec.
   to children-Unice,Lennard Johnson Hutson,Mitchell Turner Hutson
      Littleton Robins Hutson,Peter Smith Hutson,James Parker Hutson
   wit;Cornelius Dickerson,Samuel Banks,Thomas Pennewell
   bonds include-John Williams
```

```
                            f-249-252
TOWNSEND,Leah               15 Oct 1799      4 Sep 1801
   to son-Luke, lands obtained of Major James Handy
   to sons-James and Joshua
   to dau-Eleanor Merrill
   to gr.daus-Leah Selby Merrill,Sally Merrill,Elizabeth
      Merrill
   son-John,exec.
   wit;Hanah Stevenson,John A.Townsend,William Selby
   bonds-Josiah Brattan,Jacob Teague
                            f-253-254
LONG,Coulbourn              31 Jul 1801      17 Sep 1801
   towife-Sally, lands (pregnant)
   to William Henry Lankford son of my sister Elizabeth
   wit;Jehu Watson,William Hancock, William Handcock Jr.
                            f-255
HENDERSON,Jacob (dec'd)                      9 Oct 1801
   Adm.bonds by Matthew Dorman,William Dorman,Parker J.Dorman
                            f-255-256
SELBY,Daniel    dec'd)                       13 Oct 1801
   adm.bonds by James Sellby,Parker Selby,Robert M.Richardson
                            f-256
TIMMONS,Caleb, dec'd                         14 Oct 1801
   adm.bonds by Thomas Timmons,Stephen Purnell,Starling Jones
                            f-257-258
PRICE,Thomas                22 Jun 1788      16 Oct 1801
   to wife-Patience, land 50a. MtPLEASANT,exec. then to
   son-Solomon Kibble Price
   to sons-George Tebbles Price, Louther Price
   wit;Jacob Morris,Jacob Morris Jr.,Joshua Tyalor,George
      Matthews, John Harris Hayman
                            f-259-260
RICE,George                 8 Apr 1798       23 Oct 1801
   to wife- Mary Ann, the policy in effect on the Brig Polly
      and ½ cargo when it returns. Storehouse on lands in
      Snow Hill belonging to Robert Dennis. She to pay debts
      due in Philadelphia
   to only son-Walter Rice, minor
   wit;Walter Smith,Robert Smith
   bonds include-Robert M.Richardson,Samuel R.Smith
                            f-261-262
JOHNSON,Alice               5 Jul 1801       30 Oct 1801
   to gr.dau-Betsy Johnson dau/of John Shockley
   to gr.dau-Alice Johnson dau/of William Cottingham
   to daus-Ebe Shockley and Polly Cottingham
   to gr.dau-Patty dau/of Smith Johnson
   to children-Henry Johnson,Shepherd Johnson,Eliazer Johnson,
      Smith Johnson, John Johnson
   wit;Benjamin Dennis,Wheatley Dennis,James Dennis
```

```
                              f-263-264
RACKLIFFE,Sarah          15 Oct 1801      25 Nov 1801
   3 lots #8,9,10 in Square 165 in City of Washington
   conveyed me by Benjamin Stoddert on Pennsylvania Avenue.
   to son-Rider Henry Rackliffe, pt. lot #9
   to son-John, pt. lot #9
   to dau-Charlotte Rackliffe, lot#8
   to dau-Kitty Henry Rackliffe, lot #10
   wit;Levin Irving,Matilda Handy,Dorothy Anietta Winder
   bonds-Zadock Sturgis,Edward H.Rounds in presence of
     Mathew Hopkins
                               f-265
RACKLIFFE,John, dec'd                      25 Nov 1801
   adm.bonds by William Winder,Zadock Sturgis,Edward H.Rownd
                               f-265
SELBY,James of Jno. dec'd                  8 Dec 1801
   adm.bonds by Polly Selby,John Selby of Parker,Benjamin Gunby
                               f-266
SELBY,Anne, dec'd                          8 Dec 1801
   adm.bonds by Polly Selby,John Selby of Parker,Benjamin Gunby
                               f-267
SELBY,Daniel, dec'd                        8 Dec 1801
   adm.bonds by Peter S.Corbin,William Corbin,Thomas Slocomb
                               f-267
PETTITT,Esther, dec'd                      15 Aug 1801
   I Anne Pettitt dau/of Esther renounce administration
   bonds-8 Dec 1801 by John Bishop,Zadock Sturgis,Jacob Teague
                              f-268-271
BAYNUM,William           8 May 1800       8 Dec 1801
   to wife-Zipporah, plantation and 1/3rds
   to son-Belitha, plantation where I now live
   to son-James, 50a. pt. of STRIFE e/s Nassango Creek adj.
     Henry McGee
   to son-William, bal. of STRIFE,116a.
   to dau-Molly Freeman and gr.son Ananias Freeman
   to dau-Zeporah Davis and gr.dau. Betsy Davis
   to son-Elisha
   wit;Isaac Evans,Zadock Powell,Belitha Powell
   bonds inc. John Williams,Belitha Baynum,John Davis
                              f-271-272
DRYDEN,Jane(Jenny)       7 Mar 1797      no prob.date 1801
   to son-Sewell
   to gr.daus-Polly Dryden,Sally Dryden,Betsy Dryden
   to gr.sons-John Dryden, Samuel Dryden
   wit;George Purnell, John Jones
                               f-273
SCARBOROUGH,John Jr.      1 Aug 1801
   to wife-Elizabeth,plantation where I live, land bou/o
     Kendal Scarborough TIMBER QUARTER
   Having no sons- Jessee Bennitt, exec.
   wit;Eleanor Truitt,Sally Smullin,William Bennett
                              f-274-276
DAVIS,Ezekiel           20 Jul 1801        9 Jan 1802
   to dau-Leah Davis
   to nephew- John Walker. brother-in-law-John Walker,exec.
   wit;Thomas P.Rackliffe,John Smith Morris
   bonds inc. Edward Davis
```

                        f-278
SCARBOROUGH,John of Samuel dec'd   6 Jan 1802
    adm. bonds by Zadock Selby,Purnell Hill,Jesse Bennett

                        f-277
HOLLOWAY,Ebenezer, dec'd.   8 Jan 1802
    adm.Bonds,Jedida Holloway,Joseph Holloway,James Selby
    of Ezekiel.

                        f-279
IRONSHIRE,Esther, dec'd   29 Jan 1802
    adm.Bonds by James Franklin,William Riley,William Parker

                        f-283
TOWNSEND,James s/o Danford 16 Apr.1792   10 Feb.1802
    to wife Mary 50 acres,pt. PORTERS DISCOVERY, deeded me
    by my fahther Danford Townsend, 15 acres same deeded
    me by my nephew Danford Townsend. Executor
    wit;William Handy, Thomas R. Handy,Comfort Handy

                        f-284
TIMMONS,Samuel   24 none 1802   12 Feb1802
    to wife Leah, lands, after her death to
    son-George 10 acres
    to 5 shildren, Rebecca Smyth, Sarah ⁺argro, Mary Birch,
    Annanias Timmons, Leah Timmons, Riaah Timmons
    dau-Leah Timmons, exec.
    wit; Peter Long, Purnell Williams

MORRIS,Edward Rownds, word of mouth - f-286
    4 Sep.1801   12 Feb 1802
    said to George Martin, that any property to be
    divided between the following relatives.
    to John Rownd of Lame Rownd, his uncle
    to Henry Rownd of Lame Rownd, his uncle
    to Martha Rownd, and Ann Rownd
    to William Morris and James Morris of James R. Morris
    uncle on Bristol #4.
    wit:Increase Blake of Boston,Reuben Bunker of Hudson
    George Martin of Baltimore (Capt.)

f-287
TAYLOR,Thomas, dec'd   5 Mar 1802
   adm.bonds by Rebecca Taylor,Hezekiah Johnson,Michael Tarr
                     f-288-289
DIKES,William   7 Jan 1802   5 Mar 1802
   to son-Daniel, land in forest,WILLIAMS CHOICE
   to wife-Sarah, pt.tr.TRUITTS HARBOR pur/o Samuel Truitt,exec.
   wit;Samuel Johnson,Samuel Truitt,Boaz Ennis
                     f-290-292
PREWIT,William   24 Sep 1798   15 Mar 1802
   to wife-Anne, the GRAVE YARD PLACE after decease to son
     Charles. Corn & fodder William Slocomb tends
   to son-Charles, plantation, exec.
   to son-Fisher
   to dau-Esther Prewitt
   to sons-Wlater and Elijah, 1 sh.each
   to dau-Attalanter, 1sh.
   wit;John Holland,Ezekiah Johnson,John Prewitt
                     f-293-294
BOWEN,John   21 Feb 1802   12 Mar 1802
   to children-James and Ledia (minors)
   brothers-Elisha Bowen,Nathaniel Bowen gdns, execs.
   to Robert Henderson, joiner tools
   wit;Thomas S.Fassitt,William Bowen,Sarbra Bowen, Sarah Bowen
   bonds inc-Edmond Crapper,Curtis Henderson
                     f-295-296
MARTIN,Nanny   12 Dec 1801   6 Apr 1802
   to two children-Joseph Bishop and Denny Bishop
   to gr.son-William Bishop Smith
   wit; Jacob Teague,Elizabeth G.Conner,Elizabeth Bishop Conner
                     f-297-299
TIMMONS,Thomas   30 Sep 1797   14 Apr 1802
   to sons-Benjamin, Stephen, Bassitt, lands DOUBLE PURCHASE
     and STRABANE, 140a.
   to son-Benjamin,37½a. pt. afsd.near SMITHS INDUSTRY and then
     to his son Thomas
   to son-Bassitt, 51a. pt.afsd.trs.;estate that fell to him
     from his grandfather John Bassitt, dec'd), exec.
   to son-Stephen, 51a. adj. my brother Stephen Timmons, exec.
   to dau-Mary Moore and gr.son Thomas Moore
   wit;Bartholomew Slattery,Joseph Timmons,Isaac Gray
                     f-300
HUDSON,James H.,dec'd   23 Sep. 1802
   adm.bonds by Robert Hudson,Levi Hudson,Edmond Crapper Sr.
                     f-301
WILSON, James Dr., dec'd   23 Apr 1802
   adm.bonds by Joshua Prideaux,Jacob White,John J.Williams
                     f-302
WARREN,John, dec'd   1 May 1802
   adm.bonds-Ledia Warren,William Hall,Annanias Jarman

```
                        f-303
PURNELL,John, dec'd                    21 May 1802
   adm.bonds-Betsy Purnell,Thomas M.Purnell,George W.Purnell
                        f-303-304
CRAPPER,Noble           14 Apr 1802    4 May 1802
   to wife-Eleanor,exec.
   to all five children, unnamed
   wit;Elisha Davis,Peter Whaley,Jessee Davis
                        f-305
HENDERSON,William       2 Apr 1800     17 May 1802
   to gr.son-William Henderson, pt.tr.DOUBLE PURCHASE where
      Sally Henderson lives (desc) bounds Wm.Fadry?Adams
   to dau-Sinah Slocomb, bal.of land afsd., exec.
   to gr.sons-Noah Henderson,Henry Slocomb,Levin Henderson
   to son-Noah Henderson
   to dau-Leah Henderson and her children
   to gr.daus-Ann Henderson, Sally Slocomb
   to daus-Ann Henderson,Nancy Henderson
   Joseph Henderson, exec.
   wit;Joseph Houston,Levi Henderson,William F.Adams
                        f-308-311
CATHELL,David           16 Feb 1802    7 May 1802
   to son-Joshua, tr.land bou/of Saul Davis dec'd, tr.MILL
      LOT, 325a.,½ of lot in Salisbury Town
   to son-James Tompson Cathell, tr.ADDISHEN TO PRISTON 400a.
      bond for 50a. from David Cathel dec'd, ½ lot in Salisbury
   to brother-John Cathell, 79a. adj.pt. SAFE GUARD where
      Thomas Henington lives DAVIDS OUTLET, exec.
   to brother-Levi Cathell-42a. out of CATHELLS CHANCE adj.
      GEORGES PURCHASE
   bal.of DAVIDS OUTLETT,CATHELLS CHANCE,MARKET RIDGE be sold
   wit;Thomas Fooks,James Fooks of Thos.,Nathan Parsons
   bonds-include Eben Christopher,Samuel Hilman
                        f-312
TIMMONS,Thomas, dec'd                  7 May 1802
   adm.bonds-Bassitt Timmons,Elzey Smith,Leonard Timmons
                        f-312-313
MORRIS,Edward Rownd                    12 May 1802
   adm.bonds-Samuel McMasters,William Stevenson,Littleton Robins
                        f-313-315
STEVENSON,Joseph of Joseph 22 Dec 1798  14 May 1802
   to wife-Molly
   to dau-Betty
   to son-Edward, lands (desc)bounds Thomas Harris, exec.
   to son-Joseph, lands
   wit;Hugh Nelson,Levi Ball,Thomas Harris
                        f-316
BRATTAN,John S.,dec'd                  19 May 1802
   adm.bonds-Mary Ann Rice,Samuel R.Smith,Zadock Sturgiss
                        f-317-8
HENDERSON,William, dec'd               19 May 1802
   Joseph Henderson rejects adm.
   adm.bonds-Sinah Slocomb,John A.Slocomb,Bayley Young
```

                         f-318
WILLIAMS,Isaac,word of mouth on 17 May 1802   25 May 1802
   to dau-in-law-Peggy Williams
   to-Charlotte Breyer
   to gr.son-Thomas Purnell Williams
   to-Purnell Fletcher Smith
   wit;Luke Teeling,Thomas Taylor,Thomas M.Purnell
                         f-319
KNOX,Ezekiel, dec'd   28 May 1802
   adm.bonds-Barnabas Henderson,Curtis Henderson,Benjamin Bishop
                         f-320
WILLIAMS,Isaac ,dec'd   9 Jun 1802
   adm.bonds-Peggy Williams,Levin Mitchell,James A.Collins,
      Stephen Purnell
                         f-320
McGIVERAN,John dec'd   9 Jun 1802
   adm.bonds-John Bowhannan,Samuel McMaster,Zadock Selby
                         f-321
CRAPPER,Noble,dec'd   20 Jun 1802
   adm.bonds-Eleanor Crapper,William Hammond Sr.,Barzilla Parker
                         f-322
GIBBS,John   6 Apr 1802   12 Aug 1802
   to wife-unnamed
   wit;William Corbin,John Cotittingham,James Broadwater
                         f-323-330
GUY,Major   12 Aug 1796   11 Aug 1802
   to daus-Elizabeth(Betty)Selby, Nanny Guy
   to son-Major Guy, lands, dau.Betty to live with him.
   to dau-Joanna Sturgis
   to gr.dau-Nanny Jones,furniture intended for her mother
   to gr.daus-Sarah Sturgis,Nanny Sturgis
   wit;Peter Spencer Corbin,William Holland Jr.,John Shepherd Ker
   codicil 16 Dec 1800(changes wording of will)
   wit;John McLean,William Welbourn,John S.Ker
   codicil 14 Jun 1802
   to- Catharine Spicer
   also eliminated dau.Nanny, ments.prop she gave him
   wit;John Holland,James Jones,Joseph Davis
                         f-331-332
PERDUE,John Sr.   25 Jun 1802   12 Aug 1802
   to son-George, lands (desc), exec.
   to sons-James and Louder
   to daus-Sabra Perdue(exec) and Matty Perdue
   wit;Moses Parks,Frederick Perdue,Loudy Christopher
   bonds include-John Tingle
                         f-334
FASSITT,Rouse, dec'd   8 Aug 1802
   adm.bonds by-Thomas S.Fassitt, Zadock Purnell,Thomas Purnell
                         f-335-337
NEWBOLD,Thomas   12 Aug 1800   30 Aug 1802
   to wife-Mary,plantation, exec.
   wit;Joshua Prideaux,William McCrea,Thomas Purnell
   adm.bonds-Nancy Kirby (adm),Thomas N.Williams,Jacob White

```
                        f-338-9
ROWNDS,Mary            15 Jun 1802     3 Sep 1802
  to gr.daus-Mary M.Teagle, Sally Quinton
  to nephew-William R.Turpin (under 20)
  to neice,Eliza J.Williams
  wit;Jacob White,Isaac Long
  bonds inc-Sally Quinton,William R.Warwick,Jacob White
                        f-340
RIGSBY,Thomas, dec'd                   24 Sep 1802
  adm.bonds-Milby Purnell,Esme Purnell,Curtis Henderson
                        f-341
TOADVINE,William,of John, dec'd        8 Oct 1802
  adm.bonds-Charity Toadvine,Johnson Hayman,Jonathan Owens
                        f-342-343
DENNIS,Littleton       19 Sep. 1802    12 Oct 1802
  to brother-James Dennis,exec.
  wit;John McCalley,William Townsend
  bonds include-Levin Conner,Jesse Riggen
                        f-344
PURNELL,Elisha Esq. of Wm.             14 Oct 1802
  adm.bonds-Sally Purnell,Littleton R.Purnell,L_ittleton Robins
                        f-345
COLLINS,Walton,dec'd                   22 Oct 1802
  adm.bonds-James Selby of Eze.,Zadock S_turgis,Ephraim K.Wilson
                        f-346-347
DIXON,Ambrose          1 Jan 1800      22 Oct 1802
  to wife-Nelly, 1/3 lands, exec. (may be pregnant)
  to sons-Nathaniel,Samuel,Outterbridge, lands be divided
  to daus-Betty,Nancy,Nelly
  wit;William Richardson,William Dixon,Samuel Dixon
                        f-348-351
PERDUE,James, planter  23 Jul 1802     27 Oct 1802
  to 3 sons-James Walker Bayley Perdue, John Kendal Hew Perdue,
     Elijah Shalby Washington Perdue (a minor)
  to daus-PollyKennett Perdue,Elizabeth Elender Young Perdue
  to-Sally Beauchamp Dennis
  to dau-Arcadia Walker Perdue, 1 sh.
  friend; George Bell,exec.
  wit;John Dennis,Joshua Trader,Elijah Beauchamp
  bonds-John Dennis of Johnson,Joshua Trader
                        f-352-354
PATTERSON,Sarah        10 Sep 1802     29 Oct 1802
  to sons-Anderson Patterson,James Patterson,John West Patterson
  to gr.son-James Patterson son of Revil Patterson dec'd pro-
     vided his mother Sarah Waggaman gives him a bond I gave
     his father
  wit;Hanah Morrison,Leah Goslee
  bonds include-George Patterson
```

```
                          f-355-357
SELBY,Levin            8 Nov 1802      19 Nov 1802
   to daus-Easter Selby,Elizabeth Selby
   to son-Levin Selby (under 21)
   lands in Mattaponi 100 to be sold 70 1/3a.CANOGANA-
      STICK bou/of George Johnson & Micajah Johnson
   to sister-Leah Tull
   bro-in-laws-John Whittington,Selby Parker, execs.
   wit;Michel Tarr,John Ayres,John Allen Sr.
                          f-358
HARRISON,John dec'd                     3 Nov 1802
   adm.bonds-Clement Turner of Caroline Co.,Esther Harrison,
      Job Newton,Eli Collins
                          f-359-362
STURGIS,Joshua         17 Sep 1802     14 Dec 1802
   to son-Joshua,lands
   to dau-Sally Sturgis, land in Somerset County
   to wife,Esther,exec.
   wit;John Cathell,Wm.Sturgis,Nancy Dixon,Stephen W.Thorns
                          f-363
CHAILLE,Peter, Col,word of mouth 6 Oct 1802 14 Dec 1802
   to wife-Scarborough Chaille
   wit;William Holland,John Gunby
                          f-364
SELBY,Levin, dec'd                     15 Dec 1802
   letter to Mr.Selby Parker from John N.Whittington dated
   24 Nov 1802- cannot adm.est.of Levin Selby
   adm.bonds by-Selby Parker,Zadock Selby,Samuel A.Harper
                          f-365
SELBY,Thomas           22 Oct 1799     30 Dec 1802
   to wife-Elizabeth Selby, exec.
   plantation to be sold
   to four daus.-Sary Selby,Cathron Selby,Martha Selby,
      Peggy Selby
   to son-Thomas,100a. formerly belonging to Easter Draper
   to son-Kendal, tr. bou/of Joseph Waters, parcel bou/of
      Annias Jarman
   to sons-James and John
   wit;William H.Taylor,Isaac Hill,Thomas Webb (he dec'd by 1802)
   bonds include-William Fassitt


                        end of this book
```

INDEX

ADAMS,William-305
ALLEN-John-355
  Stephen-209
  William-212
ADKINSON-ATKINSON
  James-166-182
  John,25
  Polly,25
  Robert-39-182
  Sarah-25
  Samuel-25
  Thomas-182
  Willliam-25
AYDELOTTE-Wm-37
AYRES-Isaac-53-183-206-221
  John-151-185-186-355
BACON-Anthony-1
  James-212
BAKER-Solomon-218
BALL-Levi-34-171-313
BANKS-Samuel-247
BARRETT-Caty-143
BASSITT-John,297
BAYNUM-Belitha-268
  Elisha-268
  James-268
  Zipporah-268
  William-268
BEACHBOARD-Malthy-241
BEAUCHAMP-Elijah-348
BELL-Henry-50
  George-10-348
BENNETT-Wm. 273
  Jesse-4-214-273-278
BENSON-John-68
  Michael-68
BENTON-John-22
BEVANS-Bathsheba-138
  Benjamin-178
  Jane-138
  Jemima-178
  Mary-178
  Mills-138
  Rowland-138
  Taby-138
BIRCH-Mary-284
BISHOP-Anna-6
  Benjamin-319
  Denny-295
  John-6-123-110-138-187-267
  Joseph-295
  Susannah-56
BLAKE-Increase-286

BOHANNON-John-151-320
BOSTON-Esau-143
BONNEWELL-John-241
BOWEN-BOWIN
  Betsy-187
  Eli-78
  Elisha-293
  Catty-187
  Hetty-187
  James-293
  John-110-187-293
  Joshua-187
  Nathaniel-117-110-293
  Riley-17
  Sabra-293
  Sarah-293
  Ledia-293
  Nathaniel-117-110-293
  Whittington-117-110-293
  William-293
BRADFORD-Avery-201
  John-203
  Sally-203
BRADSHAW-Morgan-223
BRATTAN-Cata-56
  Comfort-56
  James-159
  John-120-56-316
  Josiah-56-192-249
  Mary-120
  Nathaniel-56
BREDELL-Edward-10
BREVARD-Adam-10
  Ebenezer-10
  James-10
  John-10
  Nancy-10
  Sarah-10
BRITTINGHAM
  Elijah-106-221-224
  Isaac-184
  Joshua-197
  Nathaniel-84
  Solomon-184
BROADWATER-
  James-121-322
BROTHERY-James-74
BRUFF-Zipporah-84
BRUMBLY-Jabez-86
BUNKER-Reuber-286
BURBAGE-Thomas-17
BURTON-William-232
BUTLER-Kala-25
CAMMELL-Elizabeth-232
CATHELL-David-308
  Levi-308
  James-308

CATHELL-Joshua-308
  John-20-308-359
CHAILLE-Peter-98-363
  Scarborough-363
CHRISTOPHER
  Eben-308
  Loudy-331
CHURCH-John-232
CLARKE-Mary-281
  Elizabeth-98
COLLIER-
  Catherine-93
  George-7
  Kendal-7
  James-89
  John-7-93
  Layfield-89-106-10'
  Lambert-7
  Molly-7-89
  Peter-7
  Sally-89
  Tabitha-89
COLLINS-Eli-358
  James-320
  Walton-345
CONNER-Levin-342
  Elizabeth-295
  Frederick-185
CORBIN-Peter-234-267-323
  William-183-267-322
CORD-Nancy-10
COTTINGHAM-Alice-261
  Isaac-115
  John-166-322
  Polly-261
  William-261
COVINGTON-Wm.-229
CRAPPER-CROPPER
  Ebenezer-17
  Edmond-17-293-300
  Eleanor-303-321
  Elizabeth-17
  Emila-17
  John-17
  Josiah-17
  Noble-303-321
  Reuben-7
  Stephen-7
  Sabrina-17
  William-17
DALE-John-218
  James-218
  Jacob-281

DALE-Thomas-218
　William-232
DAVIS-Abisha-203
　Abijah-101-182
　Betty-101
　Betsy-10-268
　Charles-234
　Benjamin-101
　Edward-274
　Elisha-303
　Ezekiel-117-274
　Hetty-10
　Isaac-101
　Jessee-303
　John-10-181-122-268
　Joseph-323
　James-37-117
　Littleton-101-182
　Major-171
　Nancy-234
　Leah-274
　Rachel-237
　Sarah-10
　Saul-308
　Stephen-20
　William-37
　Zepporah-268
DENNIS-Benjamin-153
　James-342
　John-93-348
　Johnson-348
　Littleton-143-342
　Sally-348
　Vollentine-179
　Wheatly-182
DERICKSON-Levin-198
DEVERIX-William-194
DICKERSON-Betsy-189
　Cornelius-247
　Elisha-289
　John-189
　James-133-26-189
　Peter-189
　William-189
DIKES-Daniel-288
　Sarah-288
　William-288
DIXON-Ambrose-346
　Betty-346
　Mary-109
　Nancy-346 -359
　Nathaniel-346
　Nelly-346
　Outterbridge-346
　Samuel-346
　Thomas-98
　William-346

DORMAN-Levi-237
　John-166
　Matthew-255
　Nehemiah-45
　Parker-255
　William-255
DOWNS-Margaret-176
　Mitchell-176
　Sarah-176-287
　Robert-176
DRAPER-Easter-365
DRYDEN-Jane-171
　Jenny-271
　Betsy-271
　John-271
　Polly-271
　Sewell-271
　Samuel-271
DUER-James-153
DUKES-Thomas-65
DUNBAR-Joseph-53
DURHAM-Johnson-187
ELMORE-Comfort-132
　John-132-235
ENNIS-Samuel-184
ESHOM-Sally-6
EVANS-Hannah-26
　Isaac-268
　John-74
　Joshua-74
　Pett-65
　Peter-236
FASSITT-Elizabeth-44-93
　James-10-44-93
　John-93
　Rouse-7-334
　Thomas-7-43-293-334
　William-93-365
FOOKS-James-308
　Thomas-308
FRANKLIN-Alexander-44
　Comfort-232
　Ebenezer-232-236
　Isaac-236
　James-236-279
　Robert-232
　Sarah-232
　William-232
　Freeman-Ananias-268
　Molly-268
GIBBS-John-322
GILLETT-Anna-171
　Elizabeth-171
　John-98
　Wealthy-171
　William-171
GIVEN-John-151

GODFREY-Anna-197
GLASS-Christopher-241
GORE-Comfort-123
GORNELL-Major-194
　Sally-194
　Mary-194
GOSLEE-Leah-352
GRAY-Isaac-297-13
　Jessee-237 -50
　Johnson-180
　Littleton-50
　Martha-180
　Thomas-180
GREEN-Joseph-43
　Mary-43
GREYER-Charlotte-318
GREER-Moses-208
GUMBY-Benjamin-265-266
　John-363
GUNN-Betsy-39
　George-98-39
　Henry-98
　Levin-98
　Mary-98
　Rebekah-98
　Samuel-116-39
GUY-Major-323
　Nanny-323
HADER-Betsy-241
HALL-David-68
　George-187
　Katherine-68
　Elizabeth-74-217
　George-187
　Thomas-187
　William-302
HAMMOND-Edward-17
　Joshua-22
　William-321
HANDCOCK-Daniel-241
　John-207-222
　Sally-241
　William-254
HANDY-Comfort-283
　Elizabeth-1
　Esther-1
　George-1
　Jacob-212
　John-120-182-212-246
　Levin-1
　Matilda-263
　James-1-280-287
　Prisse-1
　Richard-112-113
　Robert-189
　Samuel-115-153-212
　Sarah-1

HANDY-Thomas-112-113-
    121-166-283
  William-25-138-283
HARGIS-Thomas-34
HARGRO-Sarah-284
HARPER-Samuel-47-364
HARRIS-Thomas-313
HARRISON-Esther-358
  Erasmus-198-203
  John-358
  William-237
HAYMAN-Cornelius-20
  John-20-257
  Johnson-341
  Tabitha-20
  Nehemiah-20
HAYWARD-George-182
HEATHER-John-78
HENDERSON-Aary-226
  Ann-305
  Barnabas-319
  Betty-143
  Curtis-197-293-319-
    340
  Easher-226
  Elizabeth-226
  Isaac-198
  James-226
  Jacob-226-255
  Joseph-143-309-317
  Levi-226-305
  Levin-305
  Leah-305
  Nancy-198-305
  Noah-305
  Robert-293
  Sally-305
  Purnell-198
  Thomas-198
  William-305-317
HENINGTON-Thomas-308
HENRY-Edward-89-84
HILL-Betsy-217
  Elizabeth-229
  Elijah-89
  Frederick-209
  Isaac-89-224
  Jesse-217
  John-217
  Josiah-89
  Levin-209
  Levina-209
  Nancy-217
  Peggy-209
  Purnell-209-214-278
  Stephen-89
  William-74-217

HILMAN-Samuel-308
HINEMAN-James-235
HOLLAND-Leah-17
  Elizabeth-119-118
  John-119-118-241-290-
    323
  Nehemiah-234
  Thomas-119-33
  William-234-323-363
HOLLOWAY-Ebenezer-277
  Jedida-277
  Joseph-277
HOLSTONE-Ralph-159
HOOK-McKimey-17-83
  Robert-159
  William-159
HOPKINS-Matthew-263
HORSEY-Isaac-22
  Lambert-84
  Outerbridge-22
  Patty-22
  Revil-84
HOUSTON-George-214
  James-126
  John-214
  Joseph-189-246
HUDSON-HUTSON
  Caleb-53
  Hannah-32
  James-247-300
  Jesse-68
  John-247
  Leonard-247
  Levi-59-30-300
  Mitchell-247
  Littleton-247
  Peter-247
  Polly-247
  Robert-117-300
  Sally-39
  Unice-247
  William-7
HUGHES-Hannah-4
  James-4
  Jessee-4
  John-4
  Martha-4
  William-4
HULL-Catherine-110
  Richard-110
INGERSON-John-15
IRONSHIRE-Esther-279
  William -229
IRVING-Levin-263
JACOBS-Nimrod-33-118
JARMAN-Ananias-198-
    302-365

JOHNSON-Alice-261
  Denny-53
  Eliazer-261
  Elisha-86
  Ezekiah-86-290
  George-355
  Henry-261
  Hezekiah-86-287
  John-261
  Laban-93
  Micajah-355
  Nicy-208
  Patty-261
  Shepherd-261
  Smith-261
JONES-Charlotte-78
  Handy-78
  James-224-323
  Jesse-78
  John-93-224-271
  Mary-26
  Major-26
  Nanny-323
  Polly-78
  Rebecca-78
  Riley-78
  Starling-256
  Thomas-132
KENNERLY-John-101
KER-John-323
KILLAM-Nancy-56
  Joseph-278-287
KING-James-50-180
KIRBY-Ann-37
  Nancy-335
KNOX-Ezekiel-319
  Solomon-22
LAMBDEN-Edward-226
LANKFORD-Elizabeth-254
  William-254
LAWRENCE-John-13
LAWS-Comfort-132-224
LAYFIELD-Esther-143
  Isaac-143
  Nancy-143
  Thomas-143
LOGAN-John-171
LONG-Coulbourn-254
  Isaac-338
  Peter-284
  Sally-254
MADDUX-Charlotte-138
  Marcey-280
  Sally-138-280
MARCHMENT-Riley-278
MARINER-Constant-93
  Comfort-93

MARSH-Phillip-20
MARSHALL-Elizabeth-46
  Jephtat-126
  John-46-112-113-143
MARTIN-Anna-153
  Charlotte-153
  George-153-286-287
  James-114-153-286
  Leah-153
  Levin-153
  Molly-153
  Mary-153
  Nanny-295
  Rossanah-114
  Sarah-153
  Susan-153
  Thomas-114-153-212
  William-153
MASSEY-John-37
  Priscilla-93
MATTHEWS-Ephraim-47
  George-257
MELVIN-Jonathan-133
  Sarah-133
MERRILL-Eleanor-249
  Elizabeth-249
  James-138
  Leah-249
  Levi-4-278
  Sally-249
  Samuel-226
MEZICK-Anna-50
  George-10-50
  Sally-50
MILBOURN-John-65
  Nancy-65
  Ralph-65
  Thomas-65
MILLER-Levin-7
MILLS-Elizabeth-34
  Gillette-34
  Handy-217
  John-34
  Levin-34
  Sarah-178
  Stephen-178
MITCHELL-Ann-229
  Josiah-89-229
  Joshua-229
  Levin-229-320
  Thomas-123-83-194
MOORE-Ann-22
  George-22
  John-22
  Mary-22-297
  John-22
  Thomas-297
  William-22

MORRIS-Ann-286
  Cornelius-201
  Edward-286-312
  James-1-286
  Jacob-257
  John-274-286
  Lame-286
  Martha-286
  Phillip-78
  William-286
MORRISON-Hannah-352
MUMFORD-Littleton-192
  Major-44-93
McALLEN-Arthur-223
  Alexander-22-223
McCALLEY-John-342
McCORMACK-Benjamin-237
McCREA-Samuel-203
  William-335
McGEE-Henry-268
McGIVERAN-John-320
McLEAN-John-323
McMASTER-Samuel-39-
  34-171-312-320
NAIRNE-Robert-20-46-280
NEILL-John--1-114-153-59
NELSON-Hugh-74-313
NESBIT-Samuel-68
NEWBOLD-Mary-335
  Thomas-335
NEWTON-Charlotte-214
  Comfort-214
  Job-358
  Josiah-214
  Levin-214
  Nancy-214
  Polly-214
  Sally-214
  Sarah-214
NICHOLSON-Joseph-115
  Isaac-45-189-246
  Nancy-189
  Samuel-109-45-115
  189
OWENS-Jonathan-341
PARKER-Barzilla-78-321
  Elizabeth-74-224
  Comfort-224
  James-224
  Mary-74-209-224
  Peter-132-224
  Selby-74-197-355-364
  William-30-279
PARKS-Moses-331
PARSONS-Nathan-308
PATRICK-John-105
  Sarah-105

PATTERSON
  Anderson-143-352
  George-352
  John-352
  Mary-143
  James-352
  Revil-352
  Sarah-352
PENNEWELL-John-221
  Rachel-221
  Thomas-247
PEPPER-Annie-241
  John-241-
  Solomon-241
  William-241
PERDUE-Arcadia-348
  Elijah-348
  Elizabeth-348
  Frederick-331
  George-331
  James-331-348
  John-331-348
  Matty-331
  Louder-331
  Polly-348
  Sabra-331
PETTITT-Ann-267
  Esther-267
PHILLIPS-Isaac-201
  Joshua-201
  Ruth-201
PILE-Samuel-232
PILCHARD-Levi-26
PITTS-Esther-218
  Hillary-218
POLLITT-Levin-182
PORTER-Purnell-187
  McKimmy-212
POSTLY-John-53-203-218
POWELL-Amercus-106
  Annias-229-237-281
  Belitha-203-237-268
  Elisha-237
  Elizabeth-237
  Esther-203
  Jesse-202-237
  John-202-203-218
  Keziah-203
  Molly-203
  Milby-237
  Rachel-237
  Samuel-218-237
  Thomas-218-237
  Zadock-237-268
POYNTER-Jean-137
  Hannay-138
PREWIT-Anne-290
  Attalanter-290

PREWIT-Charles-290
  Esther-290
  Elijah-290
  Fisher-290
  John-290
  Walter-290
  William-290
PRICE-Arthur-86
  George-257
  John-86
  Louther-257
  Patience-257
  Sarah-86
  Solomon-257
  Thomas-257
  William-86
PRIDEAUX-Joshua-84-53-301-335
PRUITT-Betsy-209
PURKINS-Polly-281
QUILLAN-Phillip-189
  Samuel-93
  William-189
PURNELL-Azariah-181
  Benjamin-46
  Betsy-303
  Elizabeth-126
  Elisha-59-126-159-186-344
  Esme-126-340
  Euphemia-176
  George-39-116-59-108-138-208-271-303
  Gertrude-176
  Henrietta-59
  John-17-20-43-59-303-108-159-186
  Littleton-59-159-344
  Lanta-108
  Martha-126
  Mary-126-181-186
  Sarah-126
  Stephen-93-256-320
  Milby-126-340
  Sally-59-344
  Thomas-17-59-303-318-334-335
  William-159-344
  Zadock-334
QUINTON-Esther-123
  Isaac-123
  Littleton-123
  Phillip-109-123
  Sally-338
  Sarah-123
  William-109-123-246
RACKLIFFE-Charlotte-263
  John-263

RACKLIFFE-John-265
  Kitty-263
  Rider-263
  Sarah-263
  Thomas-274
REDDEN-Eleanor-241
  Hetty-241
  James-133
  John-133-241
  Leah-133
  Mary-133
  Nehemiah-133-241
  Peter-241
  Sarah-241
  Shadrack-133
  Stephen-133-241
  William-241
RENNOLDS,Sarah-17
RICE-George-120-259
  Mary Ann-259-326
  Walter-259
RICHARDS-Elijah-194
  Isaac-198
  Jacob-138-280
  John-181-235
  Joseph-138
  Nathaniel-138
  William-237
RICHARDSON-
  Benjamin-192
  Fisher-179
  Levi-159-192
  Joseph-192
  Mary-56
  Robert-33-153-255-259
  Thomas-159
  William-346
RIGGEN-Jesse-342
  John-166
RIGSBY-Thomas-340
RILEY-William-279
ROACH-Stephen-50-226
ROBERTS-John-15
  Nelly-15
  Rencher-15
  Silvanus-166
  Thomas-15
  Underwood-15
ROBINS-James-22-78-159
  Littleton-108-59-30-192-312-344
ROCK-John-120
  Mary-229
ROSS-Francis-212
  George-93-121-68-212
ROUND-ROWNDS
  Edward-263-265
  John-112

ROWNDS-Mary-338
  Peggy-113
ROWLEY-Arthur-37
  Richard-37
SAMPSON-Richard-203
SCARBOROUGH-
  Elizabeth-273
  John-273-278
  Kendal-273
  McKimmy-153
  Samuel-278
SCOTT-Joseph-25
SELBY-Cathron-365
  Easter-355
  Kendal-365
  Martha-365
  Peggy-365
  Sary-365
  Thomas-365
  Ann-20-266
  Daniel-255-267
  Elizabeth-323-355-365
  George-20-39
  James-20-86-159-255-265-345-365
  John-20-118-119-45-18-265-266-277-365
  Levin-355-364
  Parker-74-183-255-165-266
  Polly-265-266
  Sally-74
  Tabitha-74
  William-20-39-189-249-246
  Zadock-74-151-278-320-364
SHOCKLEY-Betsy-261
  Ebe-261
  John-261
SLATTERY-Bartholomew-19
SLOCOMB-Henry-305
  John-317
  Sally-305
  Sinah-305-317
  Thomas-267
  William-290
SMITH-Elzey-312
  Elizabeth-53
  David-217
  James-98
  John-53
  Patty-53
  Purnell-318
  Robert-153-259
  Samuel-153-259-316
  Walter-259
  William-98-295

SMOCK-Henry-22
 Mary-4
SMULLEN-SMULLING
 Sally-273
 William-47
SMYTH-Rebecca-284
SNEED-Elizabeth-143
SPENCE-Adam-159
 Ara-159
 Betsy-159
 Andasia-159
 George-78-59-159-192
 James-159
 John-159
 Lemuel-159
 Mary-22
 Nancy-159
 Sarah-22
 Thomas-59-159
 William-159
SPICER-Catherine-323
STARLING-Hannah-26
 Joseph-26
 Southy-26
STEVENS-Eliner-121
 John-56
STEVENSON-Adam-6
 Betty-313
 Edward-313
 Hanndah-249
 John-56
 Joseph-122-171-313
 Jabez-208
 Lydia-122
 Jonathan-122
 Molly-313
 Nanny-208
 Samuel-56
 Thomas-208
 William-122-312
STODDERT-Benjamin-263
STURGIS-Esther-359
 John-6-74
 Joshua-209-359
 Jesse-65-47
 Joanna-323
 Nanny-323
 Richard-74-223
 Sarah-323
 Sally-359
 Shadrack-65
 Stephen-65-47-217
 William-359
 Zadock-39-116-123-110-22
  164-265-267-316-345
TARR-Israel-47
 James-47
 John-47

TARR-Levi-47
 Molly-47
 Michael-86-241-287-
  355
 Sarah-47
TAYLOR-Hope-241
 Jarman-171
 John-4
 Joshua-257
 Rachel-171
 Rebecca-287
 Thomas,209-287-318
 William-365
TEAGLE-Mary-338
TEAGUE-Jacob-74-110-
  192-249-267-295
TEELING-Luke-318
THOMAS-Stephen-363
TILGHMAN-Esther-178
 Ephraim-178
 Isacah-178
TIMMONS-Ananias-284
 Bassitt-297-312
 Caleb-256
 Benjamin-284
 Joseph-297
 Leonard-312
 Leah-284
 Riaah-284
 Samuel-284
 Thomas-256-297-312
TINGLE-Daniel-107-229
 Elijah-107
 John-107-331
TINGLEY-Samuel-68
 Sarah-68
TOADVINE-Charity-341
 John-341
 Outen-15
 William-15-341
TOWNSEND-Ann-166
 Danford-283
 Elijah-171
 Henry-178
 James-249-283
 John-219-224
 Joshua-249
 Lazarus-83
 Levin-166
 Leah-249
 Luke-249
 Mary-83-283
 Nancy-166
 Sally-166
 Sarah-166
 William-342
TRADER-Joshua-348
TRIP-James-126

TRUITT-Benjamin-197
 Eleanor-273
 Elizabeth-74
 George-74-281
 James-197
 John-194
 Lotte-197
 Levinar-197
 Mary-281
 Nehemiah-198
 Outten-74
 Patey-281
 Rownds-197
 Sarah-74
 Samuel-74
TULL-Annias-13
 Hannah-13
 Leah-355
 Levin-13
TURNER-Clement-358
 Levin-232
TURPIN-John-206
 William-338
VEAZEY-VEZEY
 Charles-222
 Mary-222
 Louthy-207
 Mary-222
 Sally-207
 Samuel-207
 Thurzey-207
WAGGAMAN-Sarah-352
WAILES-Benjamin-46
WALKER-John-274
WALTON-Nancy-179
 John-183
WARREN-Ledia-302
 John-302
WARWICK-William-338
WATERS-Esther-185
 Joseph-365
 Patrick-116-185
 Peter-185
WATSON-Jehu-254
WEBB-Thomas-281-365
WELBOURN-Wm.-323
WELCH-Sally-22
WELL-Polly-106
 Thomas-106
WHALEY-Peter-303
WHEELER,Zadock-143
WHITE-Peter-209
 Jacob-106-232-301-
  335-338
 Stephen-105
WHITTINGTON-
 William-101
 John-143-355-364

WILLIAMS-Caleb-28-32
  Edward-28
  Esau-28
  Eliza-338
  Isaac-28-318-320
  John-28-32-206-247-
    268-301
  Nancy-28
  Nathaniel-32
  Purnell-284
  Peggy-28-206-320
  Resdan-32
  Solomon-32
  Samuel-28
  Tamer-28
  Thomas-1-89-28-206-
    335
WILLIS-James-86
WILSON-David-1-176
  Ephraim-1-101-93-345
  Hugh-34
  James-17-78-301
WINDER-Dorothy-263
  William-265
WINDINGS-WINANTS
  Elizabeth-30
WISE-Betty-1-39
  Ezekiel-4-39
  Levin-153
  Molly-153
  Sarah-153
  Tabitha-39-59
  William-153
WRIGHT-Allanta-110
  Elizabeth-208
  John-110
YOUNG-Bayley-317

www.ingramcontent.com/pod-product-compliance
Lightning Source LLC
Chambersburg PA
CBHW061318040426
42444CB00010B/2693